The Strength from Within

...A Mountain of Faith

D1564603

LANA PEEK

THE STRENGTH FROM WITHIN

Sometimes it requires a mountain of Faith

Introduction

Have you been experiencing some really tough times in your life? You know, things that have seemed to punch you right in the gut and knocked you down. Are you looking for a way out or need a miracle? If so, reading this book may help you. This Memoir is a summation of some challenges in my life that took a considerable amount of Faith. Everyone talks about mustard seed faith (Luke 17:6), which means a little bit of Faith can accomplish much, but sometimes it takes a mountain of Faith because with only a little it leaves too much room for doubt, and that can change everything.

I wrote this to encourage you to be able to face whatever giants, storms or situations that may arise in your life. There is nothing new under the sun, and even though you may feel all alone, you are not. If HE did it for me, HE can surely do it for you. I have found through my experiences that GOD truly loves us, and nothing is too hard or too big for Him to accomplish if we just trust HIM.

I'm sure after reading about some of my challenging experiences you will find that your problems are not as difficult as you thought, and you can see your way through them as well. My prayer is that you find some peace and understanding for the things that you are facing.

Peace and blessings to you!!

Acknowledgments

I would like to give thanks to almighty GOD for entrusting me with this wonderful assignment and also giving me the time and patience to see it through to the end. A special thanks to my daughter, Alana Peek, for the graphics in this project. To my family and closest friends; thank you for your love, support and understanding. You made things easier for me. To all of the ones that played a part in my book, and of course in my life, I have to say thank you, because you have helped me become the person that I am today.

Dedication

I am dedicating this project to all of you who have been going through things, who are going through things and who will go through tough times, storms, trials and tribulations. This is a summation of some of my experiences that my Heavenly Father brought me through and safely across to the other shore. It doesn't matter where you come from, where you are going or even who you think you are. "For there is no respect of persons (Romans 2:11)." We all need some help every once in a while, and when there are no family members or friends that seem to be around, GOD will always be there when you invite HIM in. HE will bless you in the midst of your sin; HE will open doors that have been shut, and HE can create a way out of no way. It doesn't take a million dollars to live like a millionaire because he can and will provide all of your needs if you just trust him. In all things, lean not unto your own understanding because truly his ways are not our ways, trust him.

Whatever you are going through, don't give up. Hang on in there. Truly joy will come in the morning. Everything is not a punishment, some things are a test for your testimony. Some things are necessary to make you stronger and bring out the person that HE created you to be. When you surrender and are in HIS will, HE will take care of you.

Table of Contents

CHAPTER 1

The Early Years

I was born to a Southern Baptist Preacher and his lovely wife in 1958. I am the oldest of six children. My parents were so sure that I was going to be a boy that the only name they had picked out for me was Aaron Diaz. Much to their surprise, I was a girl! My mother had to immediately come up with another name so she chose one of her favorite TV actresses, Lana, after Lana Turner. My dad was the Pastor of a small Baptist church in Southern Pines, NC which was on the West Side (the black side of town). In the sixties, he was very active in the Civil Rights Movement. He was on the town council board and was very instrumental in bringing the different denominations and races together. He was also an English and Music teacher. My father was a good provider and made sure that we had everything that we needed. We didn't get to spend a lot of time with him because he taught out of town through the week and was involved with the church on the weekends. On some Saturday mornings, we would be awakened by the smell of homemade biscuits for breakfast. On other Saturdays, the sound of beautiful piano music would be playing in the living room. I've always loved all types of genres. Music is probably one of the most powerful tools that we have because it can change or set a mood. Music can make you feel things, remember things, and see things in a way that nothing else can do. My mother sang and had a beautiful soprano voice.

She was a housewife, but would sometimes clean other people's houses so she would have her own spending money. She always kept a clean house, made sure we had three meals a day, kept our hair neat and our clothes cleaned and pressed. She was always loving and compassionate not only to her family but to others.

I was a pretty good kid growing up. I didn't give my parents any trouble and come to think of it, neither did any of my siblings. I was far from perfect though. I got saved when I was 15 years old, and it seemed as if I got worse instead of better, but I realized that I was just growing up and was able to make some choices of my own. I quickly found out that my choices had consequences. I was sort of shy and quiet but there was still a side of me that was bold and daring. I was very passionate and dedicated to anything I got involved in. My siblings and I were very close growing up. All we had was each other because we didn't have any relatives here in NC, so our church family and friends became our extended family.

I remember one day, when I was in the third grade, one of my classmates asked me, "why are you always laughing / smiling?" Of course, at that time I was still smiling but found the smile slowly fading. I didn't know what to say. I didn't have an answer for why I was always smiling. For a long time after that, sometimes when I wanted to smile, I remembered what she said and it would wipe that grin right off my face. It was years before I realized that I was only showing how I felt and I could finally answer that question. I was laughing and smiling because I WAS HAPPY! I have learned that it's nothing wrong with expressing how you feel, especially when it's positive, because you never know who's spirit you might lift. Later, my daughter would sometimes be embarrassed if I acted silly around her, but I told her, "child, people wish they could be this free."

Since I was a PK (preacher's kid), there was a lot of pressure on me. I never wanted to do anything to embarrass my parents, even as an adult I was conscious about how my decisions would affect them. Most people thought that my siblings and I lived in a very strict home, but not really. Whatever we wanted to do, all we had to do was have all the answers to the questions like; Where are you going? Who are you going with? What time is it over? We knew what time we were suppose to be home so that was never a problem. It's funny how some people expect the preacher's children to be golden like the preacher or pastor. I know that there should be a certain standard, but I had to let some folk know that, " my daddy is the preacher, I'm not." I had to live, learn and grow as I'm sure he did. Growing up, I heard all about the "GOD of my Father," but later on HE became my GOD as well and I learned to lean and depend on HIM for myself.

CHURCH FOLK

Sistas' singin' in the choir
see each other on the street, won't speak.
Deacons lustin' after young girls
who are trying to get away from the woes of the world.

Preachers dividing the young from the old,
the rich from the poor
Sleeping with sista' Sally and Jane
and when he's caught,
It's all their fault.

Mothers testifying, but mostly lyin'
Lookin' down on the people who drink and do drugs
You know, the ones who are lost in sin
No wonder they won't come in
Oh Lord! Please have mercy on our souls
All us church folk.

-- Lana Peek

Both of my parents are deceased now. I was born on Thanksgiving day and my Mother died on Thanksgiving day, the day before my 35th birthday that year in 1992. She was 60 years old and my daughter was five. When Madea (my grandmother) passed at the age of 60, I was five. Can you see a pattern here? Well now I have reached 60 and my grandson is only three. For years my prayer has been that I live beyond 60 and one part of the pattern has already been broken.

A LETTER TO MY MOTHER

Hello Mama,

It's just me

I was sitting here reminiscing about the way things used to be.

How you loved and took care of us and showed us the way

to be good Christian girls and boys so

we would make it to Heaven one day.

I miss your sweet, sweet spirit and the

sound of your angelic voice.

Because of your example I have no other choice.

I remember your radiant smile, your beautiful face

People say I look like you but it has taken a while

for the JESUS in me to saturate my heart

and flood me like the Nile.

I have to go now, 'cause here's my ride

I'll see you again some day on the other side

So keep sweet and hold my place until we see JESUS

face to face.

Love, Lana

My natural father passed away in 2004, and I somehow saw death in a different light. When I saw that smile and a sense of peace on his face, I knew that he was with GOD, the Father that he preached about all of my life. My faith walk started early because of how he lived his life and what he instilled in me. I expected good things to happen without question or doubt. I look forward to seeing them and others again some day.

CHAPTER 2

The Price of Disobedience
My Soulmate

It was late one chilly January afternoon in 1987 when I was working at a local store, attending the jewelry counter and ringing up customers. I saw him when he first turned the corner to walk down the aisle. From the moment we laid eyes on each other our souls were connected. It was like a magnetic force, the closer he approached the more I could feel him. Never looking away our eyes stay focused on each other. If there is truly a soulmate, then surely he must be the one. He walked right up to my counter and ask me if he could check out here, and I said yes, so I rang up his few household items and he went on his way. There wasn't any conversation just a few glances and smiles. I watched him as he walked away; he turned around a couple of times either to get a second look or to see if I was watching him. I wish he had asked for my number, but since he didn't, I knew if this was meant to be, we would meet again. Maybe about a week for two later I saw him at the club. He was military and he looked good in his uniform and his dress clothes. He had beautiful hazel eyes that made me want to melt when he looked into my eyes. The line to get in the club was so long that he decided to leave without going in. We did get a chance to talk some, but still no exchange of phone numbers. About one month later we ran into each other at a convenience store that was near where I lived. Now, he finally got my number. We talked on the phone for about a month and then I asked him over for dinner and he accepted. By this time it was April.

I was in beauty school at that time and one of my classmates had been asking me to come to one of her prayer meetings, and I finally told her that I would definitely be there that Monday night. Since I promised her, and I usually do what I say, I went to the prayer service before my date that night, but when I got dressed for my meeting, I dressed for him.

When I arrived at the meeting, it wasn't just a prayer service, there was a Prophet there. She asked me who I brought with me? I said, "oh the man I'm sitting beside isn't with me." She said, "No, I don't mean him. Who did you bring with YOU?" She described the man that she saw, but I didn't have a clue what she was talking about. Later, I realized that she was talking about my soulmate because he is who I had my mind focussed on and couldn't wait to see him later. She also told me that GOD was going to give me something I asked for four years ago, not knowing that something would be the child that I had miscarried five years earlier. You see during that time, I lost my job, I had just met a nice guy that I was looking forward to getting to know and I was just feeling sorry for myself. Since I lost my job, I left Durham and went back home to Fayetteville to live with my parents for a short while just to get myself together again. One night while I was saying my prayers, I was crying in my pillow and I said, "Lord, If I only had the child that I lost, I would have someone to love and someone to love me."

When I got back home that night I was ready for my date. I had a few months to imagine what it would be like in his arms, so I was excited to have a chance to find out for real. He arrived and we ate dinner, had some wine and good conversation. The chemistry was great and so natural. Then he kissed me and when he touched me it didn't matter where he touched, I could feel it all over my body. Needless to say, we ended up in my bedroom and I tell you, for it to be the first time, it was as if we had been together forever. He knew exactly what I wanted and needed and he took his time and made sure that I was thoroughly satisfied. It was as if he had taken my order and served it to perfection. I was really looking forward to being in a relationship with him only. He left the next day to go off to jump school for a month. Two days later I found myself in a predicament.

That's when Frank got up with me and that changed the course of things. I had no intention of sleeping with anyone else, but I now know that it was necessary. You see, Frank and I had been in a relationship for more than four years, years before that and we talked about getting married. A lot of people thought that we were married, but it never happened. We lived together in Raleigh, and I got pregnant during that time and that is the miscariage I spoke of earlier. The whole circumstance was so strange because Frank and I had been broken up for years and he moved to Virginia. He came home for a visit and was determined to see me that night before going back to Virginia the next day, so I agreed. When he arrived at my apartment, he had a joint behind his ear that we shared and some wine. With that combination we ended up in the bed. The strangest thing happened though. I imagined us being in our bed in our apartment that we shared in Raleigh, and I thought, "Wow, that was some good weed!" Later, I believed that it wasn't the weed at all, it was the hand of the all mighty GOD that was fulfilling the prophecy that was spoken only two days before. GOD replaced the child that I had lost in 1981 with the child I conceived in 1987, and Frank had to be the one to make this possible. That really let me know that HE truly does love us. GOD will not only bless us in the midst of sin but HE sometimes will allow sin to be a blessing to us. At the time, I didn't realize what had just happened. It took awhile for me to understand the miracle that had taken place in order to give me one of the desires of my heart. I couldn't even really tell anyone because who would believe me?

One Sunday morning, a couple of years later, I went to a service that I wasn't planning on going to; it just happened. I was invited to go to another church that morning and I couldn't find it. So since I was already in Spring Lake, I ended up going to the church where my father pastored before he passed. A guest speaker from Maryland preached that day and told a miraculous story about Hezekiah and how he prayed and asked for years to be added to his life after the prophet, Isaiah, told him that he was going to die. He too was weeping during his prayer, GOD heard his cry, granted his request and extended his life. (2 Kings 20:1-11) The preacher went on and explained that GOD reversed time in order to grant Hezekiah's request. That's how I felt about my situation, God reversed time, sent me back in time in order to bless me. That service was confirmation for me in my situation.

By the time my soulmate returned, my period was late, I was pregnant and I wasn't sure who the father was. Before that, I didn't understand how a woman couldn't know who the father of her baby was, but I found out that it's not that hard after all, especially when it was only two days apart. I told him about the baby and then he told me about his girlfriend / fiancee that he had not spoken of before. I was so hurt, but I wasn't in any position to start placing blame on anyone about anything. He knew he had been with me so he assumed that the baby was his. He didn't ask me about anyone else. We continued to see each other but reluctantly on his part, though. He would come over and see me but would always say that it didn't mean anything or that we weren't together.

I had the baby in December, and he was on a 30 day leave and had gone home for the holidays. Needless to say, I was alone when I had her. When she was first born, her eyes were light in color, like his. He said that he didn't want to see her, but later explained that he didn't want to see her, fall in love with her, and she not be his. When he finally saw her, he had tears in his eyes. He told me that his girlfriend suggested that he have a paternity test, so I agreed to it because I wanted to be sure as well. The test was scheduled for June because she needed to be at least 6 months old before testing. Their wedding date was set for September and that would be plenty of time for any decisions to be made, I thought.

We had an argument, I don't even remember what it was about but he got so angry with me that he didn't talk to me for over a month. One night in the wee hours, I woke up like I would normally do to go to the bathroom around 3:00 a.m. I would always look out of my apartment window just kinda checking on things because there was usually a lot of activity in the parking lot, but this night, I didn't. I heard a voice telling me to look out and I was determined that I wouldn't. I laid there for a bit and then I got up, went to the bathroom and still wouldn't look outside. I got back in the bed and by now the voice was yelling at me. I couldn't even go back to sleep and after while I heard a car crank up and leave. I still didn't obey and I refused to look outside. I don't know why I was so stubborn that night. Had I looked out, I would have seen my soulmate sitting in the yard. The same voice that told me to look out, told him to come to my apartment so we could talk, but he refused to come to the door. It was the voice of GOD speaking, and we both were disobedient. Had we been able to talk, things would have been different. By the weekend, I had this panic feeling come over me that I just couldn't seem to shake, so I called on base. We didn't have cell phones yet, he wasn't there. He wasn't there the whole weekend, and I still had this awful feeling that something was wrong. First thing Monday morning I called the base again and his CO answered the phone and I asked for Sgt. D and the officer asked me, "is this Mrs. D?" I said "NO, IT'S NOT!!" My soulmate came to the phone and I asked him if he had gotten married over the weekend and he said, yes. That's what he wanted to discuss with me because she wanted to push the wedding date up, so reluctantly he did. A couple of months after that, I realized what had happened that night because again he came to my apartment, sat in the parking lot and didn't come to the door, but this night, I did look out. By the time I saw him, he cranked up his car to leave, so I ran to the door and flashed my outside light. He pulled back in and came inside, and we talked. I asked him had he come to my house before and not come in and he told me that he did; it was that night, right before he got married.

The second week in June we had the paternity test done. He had his wedding band on and the meeting was very solemn and a little awkward. After the testing was done, I dropped my daughter off at her daycare. He and I went and had lunch. He wanted to make love to me but I refused because he was married now. It took a few months for the results to come back so we didn't communicate during that time. One day I was at work and he called me, very upset. The case worker called and informed him that he was NOT the father. She told him before telling me. He was so hurt and angry, and he said things to me that I didn't want to hear. I was so sick after hearing the news that I left work and went home. It felt like someone had died. Deep down he really wanted her to be his. Again, he wouldn't talk to me and I cried the whole weekend. The next week I called him and asked him to come over because I wanted to explain. He came and listened to everything that I had to say and he understood. He never asked me if I had been with anyone else. I truly didn't know if he was the father or not but I sure was hoping he was. I just needed his forgiveness and understanding at this point. He forgave me and said that he was going to stay married especially since the baby was not his. He did want to make love to me though, he was begging. I wanted to make sure that he forgave me so I made love to him one more time, I told myself.

A few months later, I moved about an hour away, I didn't tell him where I was going nor did I tell him I was opening a beauty salon. The military sent him to Korea for a year and I had every intention of going on with my life without him. When he returned he popped up at my salon. It was a shock because I didn't think he knew where I was or even cared, but he found me. He and his wife had two beautiful children but in spite of that, for whatever reason, he would pop up either where I worked or lived. We were connected in a way that just didn't make sense. I could feel his presence before seeing him or he would come out of nowhere just when I needed him the most without prior communication. He has helped me move a few times over the years. When he did pop up, it was always in between relationships never during my relationships. Over a period of about 28 years we stayed connected. We stopped having sex after a few years and although the sex was good, it's never been about that and he was married, so we decided to leave that part out of the relationship. Years might go by without connecting, but he would always find me.

This last encounter was right about this time last year. It started up again around our birthdays, which is two days apart. He scheduled a date with me for the first time in years. He took me to a restaurant of my choice. The food was delicious and the conversation was a lot different than before. He was very open and vocal about his marriage and his feelings concerning his wife and me. It was a special time for me because now it felt like I was being included in his life. You see, He was always involved in my life, whenever he came to see me he always took time for my daughter too. There were times when he was more of a father to her than her dad was. He came to two of my special birthday celebrations and even a couple of my fashion shows. I told him that I was going out of the country for a while but it seemed to make him want to see me more because he was coming over a couple of days a week and wanting to go and do things, he was also coming over and staying very late. After I left the country, he would call and wanted to be updated with what I was experiencing so I would send pictures and tell him about my adventures.

After all these years I have experienced things in this relationship that I thought I would never do, but it's because I truly believe that GOD put us together. A lot of people think that just because they get married in a church by a preacher, it means that GOD put them together. That can't be true, because when HE does it, HE brings the people together, and gives them everything that they need for each other. It shouldn't matter where they get married or by whom. It's not about the ceremony. My soulmate once said to me, "I feel like I am addicted to you." I let him know that he wasn't. Maybe it's the anointing that GOD placed on our lives, and we chose another path. It's the same anointing that GOD would place on a preacher or someone who lays hands on the sick and they are healed. HE doesn't take back an anointing just because they messed up or sinned. If HE put us together, that's what makes it so difficult for us to stay away from each other. It has never been about the physical; it's more of a spiritual thing. It was our disobedience that kept us apart. I have since learned that obedience is better than sacrifice so when I hear the voice of GOD I will obey, because it's for my good. (1 Samuel 15:22)

My First Date After 28 Years

He called and asked if I had plans, four days in advance
I wondered if I even had a chance
A chance to start over
A chance for new
A chance to be a lover
like no other only of a few
He picked me up
Took me to one of my favorite places
The food was great
The company was better
We laughed and shared secrets from our hearts
Is this a chance for a new start?
To me, the night was perfect and I enjoyed every minute
I think he felt the same way
Cause his heart was really in it.
Sometimes I wonder if this was meant to be
What GOD has put together....
Lord have mercy on me!
Is this the beginning or is this the end
Please help me to understand
This dilemma that I'm in.

-- Lana Peek

CHAPTER 3

Matrimony

I've been married twice and have yet to have a real husband. I got married the first time at the age of 45 and I truly felt like an old maid. I thought this man really wanted and loved me and we could have a good life together. I knew at the time that I didn't love him like I had loved in the past or as much as it seemed he did, but my mother once told me that I needed a man that loved me more than I loved him and that was this case. I felt that I could learn to love him or our love would grow as time went on. I married him because he asked me.

In the beginning it seemed that we had so much in common but I was wrong. Things like music, TV shows, even goals and dreams were in question. He found out who I was and what he thought I wanted and became that. He even told me, "I'm going to do whatever it takes to win you," and that's just what he did. We had only known each other for a little over 6 months before we got married and after that he stopped pretending and let me see who he really was. On top of that he lost his job and instead of finding another one, he decided to go back to school. That meant his income was limited and now I had even more on my shoulders along with the responsibility of my daughter and her high school expenses.

In spite of all of that, GOD continued to bless us financially. Over time things got pretty bad, arguments on a regular and it was too much so we decided to split before our first anniversary. The first mistake was that we didn't take enough time to see who each other was and by me waiting so long to marry, I had to learn how to let him be the man in the relationship, you know the responsible one and he didn't have the patience for that. You see, we didn't consult GOD before considering marriage, it was just something we decided to do.

It was eight years later when I met my second husband, I thought, this is real and what love is supposed to be. I met him on one of those online sites. He contacted me first and there was something about his eyes on his profile picture that drew me in. It was a picture that only showed his upper body but I could tell that he was a large man and I was ok with that. We talked back and forth for a few days and then he wanted to meet me in person. This was on a Monday and I said let's wait until the weekend because I had a very busy schedule. He insisted on seeing me sooner because he couldn't wait until the weekend, so we agreed on Tuesday night for dinner. He told me that he had lost a lot of weight since that picture was taken so he took a picture that day and sent it to me. He looked so different, it didn't look like the same person and I looked hard to see the spark in his eyes that I saw in the other picture.

We lived a little over an hour from each other so we met at a local restaurant in my area for dinner. We met in the parking lot first and then went in together. When I first saw him, he was tall and very slim. He looked frail almost sick and sad. The conversation was pretty good and it flowed well but he seemed shy and on the quiet side. We shared some things about ourselves, our backgrounds and also some hopes and dreams. When we finished dinner he walked me back to my car and he said he would like to see me again. We had a nice hug and said good night. After the date I wondered if we had enough in common because our personalities were so different. I wasn't sure if I wanted to see him again, but over the next few days he seemed to open up more, and I felt better about things. He came to my place on that Saturday, and I fixed dinner. He said he loved it, and it put a smile on his face which was a tall order because he didn't smile much. His personality came out a little bit, so we had a good time. He told me he had been married twice before and he only had two sons. I said, good because if you had been married three times I probably wouldn't date you.

He worked as a sergeant at a prison and he was an elder in the church. He said that he always wanted to have his own church and be a pastor. He asked me if we were to marry, how did I feel about being a first lady and helping him pastor a church. I told him that I wouldn't have a problem with that because I love the Lord, and ministry has always been a part of my life, being a preacher's daughter and all. Only after a couple of months he talked more and more about marriage, so I asked the Lord to give me the love for him that I need if he was to be my husband. A couple of days later I went to a program and a man was singing "Jesus is Love" by Lionel Richie, and in that moment, I felt God's overwhelming love and then I saw my husband's face. On my way home that night, I called him and told him that I loved him and that I wanted a future with him. Shortly after we made a commitment to each other.

Not long after that my daughter became seriously ill and he was by my side day and night, whatever I needed, he even took some time off work. He couldn't help me financially, but he was there for me spiritually and physically. He was my friend and my rock. Every time any of my family came to the hospital to visit, he was there. He was there even when I couldn't be there, if I had to work.

We met in September, he asked me to marry him in December, he gave me a ring for Christmas and we married in February when my daughter got out of the hospital. We had a private ceremony with family and friends at my sister's house. My sister had the inside of the whole house decorated so beautifully, and GOD decorated the outside with the most beautiful snow I had ever seen. He even sang to me as I went down the aisle and had everyone in tears. If you didn't cry then, he had a speech that surely made you cry. He moved in to my townhouse with me and my daughter. He didn't have family or friends in our area, so it was just us. Soon after, we started Bible study out of my beauty salon, and a couple of months later we were having service on Sunday mornings. We would turn the shop into what looked like a chapel. The people that came were a few friends and family members of mine.

In April, he got very upset with my daughter over her camera and came at me about it. I was shocked at the accusation, and I assured him that she didn't think like that and it wasn't the way that he thought it was. He accused me of taking her side and I let him know, I've only known you for a minute and I've known her for over 20 years. I love you and I've got your back but not in this case because, you're wrong. Please go talk to her about it, not me. He acted like a child and said no and stormed off pouting. In about a month he did it again. This time it was about coffee. Then the next time it was about bacon or sausage. He would usually act up or start something right before we were to minister on Sunday mornings. He use to be all under me before we got married; now he barely touched me and he would be in one room and I would be in another. It seemed as if no matter what I did, he didn't like it, so after a while I wasn't free to be myself. I would second guess my decisions and be very cautious about what I said and did. The only place I felt confident was at work. It was even awkward showing affection because I didn't know if he would receive it or reject it. I felt like a prisoner in my own home.

My daughter moved out and she didn't just move out, she moved all the way to DC. It was a good thing that she left because we needed our space and so did she, but it was the way things were that bothered me and the reasons why she left. Things were already bad, then he fell at work and messed up his knee and ended up having to have knee replacement surgery. He was in a lot of pain so he took some pain medication, because of that, he wasn't able to work. His temperament got worse. He became more angry and even violent. We would have heated arguments in private and later even in public. He would get out of control, which made me out of control as well. I thought that maybe his temperament was like that because of the pain he was in or because he wasn't able to get out of the house much, but I think that's just how he was.

He was never satisfied or content. Even some of the sermons that he gave about having faith, deep down he really didn't have enough himself. I loved him, took care of him and cooked meals that he would hardly eat, and I am a good cook. He would rather have Taco Bell. About the time that he fell, I found out that I was wife number three instead of number two and he had two other minor children with that wife. I knew of her but he had a phony story behind that. There were so many lies from the beginning that he told me. I don't know how he could have expected to build a solid lasting relationship on a foundation of deceit.

We stopped having church at my salon because I told him in the beginning that I wouldn't support a mess, and that is what we had, a mess. He was very angry at first but soon became connected with another ministry which he loved. The pastor made him pastor along with herself and put me over the women's ministry. When we first went there, I shared some things with her that I was going through with him, but she ignored it and even let him teach at her bible college. I thought that she had consulted God concerning him, but I realized that wasn't the case. His knee was mending now and that allowed him to have more freedom and Independence.

He got a settlement from his accident, and things seem to be going a little better. We took a week long vacation to Las Vegas; it was nice and I was hoping maybe now things would be better and we could move forward from there. Come to find out he was cheating, no one told me, all the signs were there, and the Holy Spirit showed me some things. Later I was able to speak with his ex-wife and she confirmed everything that I thought and what the Holy Spirit had said. I didn't say a word. I wanted to make sure that I had everything that I wanted out of the settlement that was owed to me for all the sacrifices that I had made and things that I had endured. After he gave me what I asked for and he was ready to make that move, he tried to start another argument and I just told him, you don't even have to do that, if you're ready to go, just go! I told him, "Please tell your girlfriend, Thank you." Thank her for taking you off my hands. Of course he denied it, but I was right. He packed up his things that night, and went. That was the end of that! I sat down for a while after he left and the Holy Spirit said, "Get the broom," and I said, "Yes, I can sweep that negative spirit out of here." I started sweeping from his side of the bed all the way out to the front porch. The next time my daughter came by, she said, it feels different in here, and I said, "yes it does, there's peace in this house again."

Months later a minister from the church that we went to, contacted me to ask my forgiveness for what she had done. I knew about her and my husband had told her a lot of lies about me, but when he started treating her mean and cheating on her, she saw the light. I forgave her and even forgave him. We were married for two and a half years and separated for 2 years before divorcing. Some of my family and friends asked me why was I being so nice to him and I replied, "I let GOD fight my battles, he does it so much better that I could ever do."

Some people have said, you should have waited on GOD to give you a husband, or you should have consulted HIM before you married. I did, I told GOD if he was to be my husband then give me the love I need for him and HE did. I loved my husband deeply and thought that this was it, but you can't build a good solid relationship / marriage on a foundation made of lies and deceit. Marriage is hard enough all by itself; it's something that you have to work on and nurture constantly. Through this experience I found out that GOD does love all of us, maybe HE loved my husband enough to bless him with another good wife just to give him one more chance to get it right, and maybe HE used me to be a blessing to my husband. Even though it was hard, it didn't kill me, and was blessed so tremendously after my marriage ended, and I am so grateful. I look forward to the REAL ONE!

CHAPTER 4

My Daughter
Blessings from GOD

My daughter's name is Alana, she was born, December 30, 1987. She's my one and only child. The one that I prayed for and GOD heard my cry and gave me one of the desires of my heart. For the first 5 years of her life, her father and his family were not a part of it. I was the only parent that she knew, so two of my best friends became her godmothers. They were the only ones who kept her when I need someone with the exception of the day care, which I loved. My mother had my niece full-time before she got sick and died. I was five when my grandmother (Madea) died at the age of 60 and when my mother died, she was 60 and Alana was five. It wasn't easy raising her on my own and in the beginning I must admit that I was afraid, mostly of the unknown but every time I needed something for her, it would show up.

I sacrificed a lot and worked really hard to provide a loving and stable home for us. Eventually, her dad and his family became a part of her life and they are very close now. She was always smart and seemed to be advanced in her learning. Her Godmother Vicky would say that she had an old soul and seemed like she had been here before. Alana would say and do things that I didn't think she knew anything about. When I asked her, "How do you know about that?" She would always say, "I just know Mama." It may sound crazy, but I will always believe that GOD placed that same seed in me that I had lost in 1981. It was prophesied to me two days before she was conceived that GOD was going to give me what I had prayed for 4 years earlier not realizing that it was the baby that I had lost. One night I was feeling down on myself because I had lost my job and because I had to move. I also lost opportunity for a relationship. During my prayer that night I was crying out to GOD because I had so much loss and I said, "Lord if I only had the child that I lost, I would have someone to love and someone to love me." I remember the night that I conceived her, I felt like I went back in time. I thought it was the pot that I smoked, but it was GOD doing the miraculous. She was an A student and after the third grade they put her in advanced classes. She played several instruments throughout middle school and High School and was on the Marching band color guard squad.

At the end of her Junior year when she was 16 and I was near the end of my first marriage, Alana got deathly ill. She was a healthy child until then. It started one Sunday after church, she took a very long nap after we got home and when she woke up her eyes were muddy brown and they stayed that way. That had never happened before. On Tuesday I had to pick her up from school because she wasn't feeling well so I took her to the doctor. They thought it was her gallbladder and set her up for an appointment two weeks later. By Thursday her eyes were yellow, I worked all day and when I got home she was so tired and kind of limp and lifeless, all she wanted to eat for dinner was green beans which she didn't eat much of. The next morning, Friday, she woke up yellow. Her eyes and skin were yellow, and she threw up a light blue liquid which they called bile. I took her to the emergency room at our local hospital and they had her there for a few hours running test, but they didn't know what was happening. Her red and white blood cells were fighting each other which was attacking her body so they gave her a blood transfusion. By the end of the day, they didn't know what to do with her so they sent her to UNC Chapel Hill Hospital. I was almost hysterical at first because I didn't know what was going on, and I was all alone.

I was in the parking lot looking for my car and I threw my hands up and screamed. After a few minutes, I got myself together and called my sister, who lived an hour away. I drove to her house and she and her husband took me to Chapel Hill which was one and a half hours away. When we got to the hospital, Alana had a team of doctors running tests and trying to figure things out. Over the weekend they ran a series of tests and ask me all kinds of questions like; Who has she been around lately, has she been out of the country recently? They thought she might have hepatitis or something and didn't know what was going on.

On Monday morning, a German female doctor discovered that she had Wilson's disease. She administered a special eye test that discovered a brown ring around the pupil of Alana's eye. This is a rare liver disease in which the copper from the foods we eat collect in the liver instead of being dispersed until it becomes toxic and usually ends in death. The doctors told me that her liver was 98 percent bad and she would need a liver transplant. I was in shock! They advised me to call my family in because she was in serious trouble, so my family and some close friends gathered at the hospital and prayed for her healing that day. During the time of our prayer my daughter was having a dream in her room, she saw her grandfather, (my father) who appeared to be a doctor. He told her that she was going to be alright because he had already fixed it. I was trusting and believing GOD for her complete healing in spite of the odds or what the doctors said.

There was some question about her insurance because I had only been with that company for less than a year, so I had to show that I had previous coverage. If I didn't have proper coverage, they couldn't do the surgery. Later that night her doctor called me and said he and the head of Blue Cross and Blue Shield attend the same church and he spoke with her and she was able to lift the Pre-existing clause. They listed her on Tuesday and had a liver and transplanted her on Wednesday. "Praise GOD!" Someone asked me if I had said, "Why me", but I replied, "No, why not me." I'm not the only person who only had one child that they could lose, nor was I too good to have to go through rough times. I was very selective about who was allowed to see my daughter because I didn't want any negative thinking or negative words spoken.

The operation went well and her color started coming back right away. She was in the hospital for two weeks, and when they released her we had to stay in a hotel nearby because they wanted her to be close. She started showing some signs of rejection so I told her to talk to her body and tell it to accept her new liver. She was in and out of the hospital a couple times for different things in relation to the transplant, but they said there would be some speed bumps along the way; that was a part of the process. She was on a lot of medication but she was alive and doing well.

In the fall Alana completed her senior year and even went to band camp in the summer. Eventually one of the bile ducts wouldn't stay open, they put a stent in to try to keep it open, but nothing worked. This liver had become sick and diseased as well. In spite of the difficulties, she went on to college at A&T University "Aggie Pride," in Greensboro, NC. She was there for three years majoring in Graphic Design. She was doing well in class, but not as well as she would have been if she wasn't sick, though. The third year before finals, she got an infection and it shut her kidneys down. She was in the hospital this time for about three weeks. I was on my way home from the hospital one night, and I got a call from my daughter. She said, "Mama guess what?" and I said, What! "I can pee!! My kidneys woke up." We were so excited! After about a week, she returned to school but A&T failed all of her classes because she wasn't able to take the final exams. She was devastated, and I was angry. They had assured me that everything was going to be fine and not to worry, but they didn't hold up their end, so she dropped out and later attended school locally at, Sandhills Community College.

In 2012 after I had met my second husband, Alana had begun to retain a lot of fluid and was gaining weight very rapidly. It was very hard for her to get around and she would get tired very easily. Her skin looked as if it would pop if she got poked. I was concerned that before long something bad was about to happen. On November 9th she woke up after midnight with a high fever. She was trembling and could hardly sit up. I called her doctor at Chapel Hill and he told me to bring her up there to that hospital. My soon- to- be- husband was still there, so he said he would take us. If he had not been there, I would have called the ambulance to pick her up because I wouldn't have been able to take her by myself, and she would have died; she was too weak to be transferred from one hospital to another like she had been a couple of times before.

The hospital is about and hour and a half from us. When we were 30 minutes out, she had to go to the bathroom really bad. By this time, it was about three o'clock in the morning, so the only places that were open were a few gas stations. We stopped, but she was in bad shape so we called the ambulance and UNC Chapel Hill picked her up. After getting to the hospital, they had to run a series of tests and they found that she was going into liver failure. After a few days while they were already trying to stabilize her, her kidneys shut down again and her blood pressure plummeted. We were about to lose her, and once again I had to call the family in because they weren't expecting her to live through the night.

They intubated her and put her in an induced coma so her body wouldn't have to fight so hard. She was in ICU, and there were people dying all around her. One of the young female doctors came to the lounge to talk to me and her sister from another mother. She told us about all of the organs that were shutting down and just how sick Alana was, so she looked at me and tilted her head to one side and said, "do you understand what I'm saying?" I told her, yes I heard what you said, but I didn't respond the way she expected. I think she wanted me to cry or scream or something. Alana's sister said, "do you mean, she's dying?" The doctor said, "yes that's what I'm saying." I just let them both know that in spite of what it looked like, I was trusting GOD. One of my close friends came in on the tail end of the conversation, and asked me, "What do you want?" I said, "I want her to LIVE," and she said, "so that's what we are going to pray for."

One of her main doctors said that if it had been anyone else besides her, they would have already been gone. The Holy Spirit told me to use frankincense and myrrh, and I added virgin olive oil for my healing oil. We anointed her and her hospital room every day. We were taking it one day at a time, and with each day she became a little stronger so she could maintain in spite of the fact that her liver and kidneys were not functioning. We were waiting for organs for one- and- a- half months. After two failed matches, she was getting tired of waiting and fighting for her life, and was about to give up. I told her to hold on and keep fighting because God had not brought her that far to leave her. "I told her to keep fighting, and I'll fight right along with you." She received her new liver and kidney on Christmas Eve.

They started the operation late December 23rd and completed the surgery on the 24th. Oh boy what a gift! What better gift than the gift of life! They left her kidneys in the back and put a new one up front. It was amazing! On December 30th we celebrated her 25th birthday right there in her hospital room with all of our family and friends. Like the first operation, I told her to tell her body to welcome her new organs so her body would not reject them. It was another month and a half before she was able to come home because her body was so weak from laying in the hospital so long. She had a feeding tube in for a while because her taste buds were off from all the medication and possibly the surgery so she didn't want to eat, and she had three drainage bags left on her. She still had to have dialysis for a few weeks and after about a month, the feeding tube was removed, and she continued to be healed. Her own kidneys even began to function again. Most of her hair came out during this ordeal, so I waited until her hair got thick enough and I cut it down, and to show my support, I cut mine as well. It took about one year for our hair to grow back to our shoulders.

The operation was a success and she hasn't really had any problems since. However, the doctors advised her not to have any children because it would be too risky, but someone prophesied to her right after her first transplant and said, "They say that you won't be able to have children, but not only will you have one child, you will have two." That prophecy has become a reality because I now have two beautiful grandchildren who are the light of my life. Over the years I have had so many miracles in my life and I AM GRATEFUL!!

It is very important for people to understand that there is much need for organ donors. A lot of people have died while waiting on a list for organs that don't exist. If you are not an organ donor, please consider being one.

CHAPTER 5

My Adventure
A life changing experience

It all began December 15, 2015, I had been feeling a certain kinda way about the way things had been going on in the US lately with all the race issues and acts of hate. Black lives matter, but yet blacks continue to kill each other and destroy their own neighborhoods. All of the confusion concerning the upcoming election. Even in my own business, the women I worked with pretending to be a friend, going behind my back talking about me and secretly wanting what I had. On top of all of that, my marriage had fallen apart. I just wanted to get away, so I told the Lord, "I don't want to be here any more so tell me where YOU want me to go."

Soon after that, I was sharing some things with a female minister friend of mine. I was telling her, when I say my prayers tonight I'm going to ask God where He wants me to go and when. While I continued to talk to her the word Peru came out of my own mouth. I was like, "where did that come from?" I quickly corrected myself and continued my conversation. For the rest of the day I heard the word "Peru, Peru, Peru" softly all day like a song playing in your head that you just can't get rid of. When I got home, I told my daughter about my day as she was watching "House Hunter" on HGTV. She said guess where the couple is from? I said, where? She said, Peru. Really I said? That's your confirmation! That night when I was about to say my prayers before going to bed, I said, Lord I would be a fool to ask you where you want me to go because you have been telling all day. Now I need to know when. The next morning I was talking to the Lord and I told Him that I needed some kind of connection when I get there, I didn't just want to go and not know anyone. The Spirit immediately replied and said "ministry". When I got to work I looked up ministry in Peru, online. There was a ministry called "The ONE Church." I thought, wow, you can't get anymore clearer than that. They had the same beliefs that I did and also had an outreach program. I continued to read and it said, "Now taking applications for Internship for Spring of 2016." There's my timeline! I was excited and everything was falling right into place. My daughter and I went right on and applied for a spot. I was surprised and very happy that she wanted to go with me. In the meanwhile, I began doing some research on Peru, it was a place that I never really considered before.

Over a period of a couple of months I had contacted "The One Church" and never got a reply. By this time, I was planning on leaving by May. My daughter asked me if we were still going even though we had not made a connection yet; this concerned me a little, but I knew GOD had me, so I said yes, we are still going. By then I knew I would go, even if I had to go by myself. A few days later, I looked up Ministries in Peru once again, this time I didn't even see The One Church, but I ran across "Peru Missions". They had the same beliefs and some American people so I contacted them. One of the pastors, Wes Baker, replied right away. He and his family are from Texas. We communicated back and forth a little more than a month, and he said that he was looking forward to meeting us. That was my contact. Praise the Lord!

You never know how much stuff you have until you move. We had accumulated so many things that we weren't even using and had forgotten about. We could only take a few personal and sentimental items with us. I sold and gave away everything like our drawings and paintings, brand new cookware, you know, just stuff. At the time I didn't know how long we would be gone but we had to have a three month return flight in place. MY daughter, my 4-month-old grandson and I were on our way. There were so many last minute things that had to be done so by the time we finally got to the airport, we had missed our flight so they re-routed us. We left Raleigh, NC, headed to Newark, NJ, to Miami to Lima Peru where customs is and then on to Trujillo Peru the next day. It took us two days!! By the time we arrived in Trujillo, it was night again and the ride from the airport was scary in more ways than one. They drive so crazy with no rules, rhyme or reason. I didn't see any traffic signs, lights, or speed limits. Some of the housing looked like shacks on the side of the road and walls were up everywhere. I thought, Oh my GOD, what have I done. In about 20 minutes we arrived in the Victor Larco area. That night we got settled in at the bed and breakfast and had a good night sleep, from our long trip.

The next morning, before I could even open my eyes, the sounds caught my attention first. Normally I might hear birds chirping, but now I hear what sounds like, owl sounds and a lot of street noise. There were horns blowing and off in the distance, music playing. We got up, had breakfast and ventured out. For a long time now, I have had a fascination for the Spanish style houses. I didn't know where that came from but those houses were everywhere, and I felt like I was home. The views were hard to describe because it was beautiful in a different way than what beautiful would mean in the US. There were people everywhere, even though there was a lot of automobile traffic, there was more foot traffic.

Education is very important to them, schools were everywhere. Later, we met up with Pastor Wes at a coffee shop which was only a few blocks away, and he invited us to church on Sunday which was within walking distance from where we were staying. I was blown away because everything we needed was all in this community and I thought, Look at GOD. I had planned to stay at the bed and breakfast for two weeks, but Victor also had apartments to rent so the next week, we went to one of his apartments. We only stayed there for a month because the furniture was very uncomfortable and the street noise was very loud. The next month we moved to a beautiful apartment that was very comfortable and quiet in a gated community. The owner's name was Carlos. He also spoke English and was very helpful.

On Sunday we went to Cristo Ray church where Wes Baker is an associate Pastor; That's where we fellowshipped the whole time we were in Peru. There was another American lady there named Alleen from Mississippi who was married to Hermes from Peru. They, along with the Bakers and some of the locals, run Peru Missions. The members of the church welcomed us with open arms. Although I couldn't speak Spanish very well, I could understand it, and my daughter was pretty fluent with it. There was a beautiful, large park, again within walking distance that we would go to. Just across the street, was a beautiful salon where we went for pedicures and pampering. The weather was wonderful, about 74 to 76 degrees during the day and about 50 degrees at night. It was Spring in the US, but Winter in Peru. Even though it was Winter, we were in Trujillo and now I know why they call it, "The City of Eternal Spring." My perfect kind of weather. It very seldom rained and there were very few insects. I loved it. There were mountain views in the background no matter what direction you looked in.

When we arrived, I didn't want to experience Peru as a tourist, but I wanted to become one of the locals and really get into their culture, so we began to familiarize ourselves with the neighborhood and our surroundings by walking to a lot of the places that we went to. There were markets and all kinds of restaurants within walking distance. When we needed a taxi, that was no problem because taxis were everywhere. All you had to do was go to the curb or the end of the road and wave your hand. They even had Uber before we did. The traffic was terrible. People drove however they wanted to. There were very few traffic lights or traffic signs on the road. Pedestrians have the right away in the US, but not in Peru. You better move out of the way or you might get run over!

During the three months we went to Haunchaco which is the beach; it was beautiful and there were a lot of Reed boats all lined up at the shore. We also visited Plaza de Armas de Trujillo which is the Freedom Monument located in the town center. We shopped at The Real Plaza, Aventura Mall and Plaza Mall Avenida Espana which was near downtown. We would go to any of the malls often, sometimes just to hang out because it reminded us of home. The cost of living is cheaper there so your money can go a long way.

We went to church on Sundays, and on Thursdays we were at Alleen and Hermes's house for Cell group which was Bible Study. There was usually at least 30 people there and the majority were young people. It was a time of fellowship and fun. We were always celebrating someone's birthday or someone coming in or going away that came in to help the Mission. I looked forward to Thursdays, and it became the highlight of my week. People asked me, what do you like most about Peru and I replied, "besides the weather, I love the warmth of the people." They greet each other with a kiss on the cheek, no matter where they are. When you run into someone that you know by chance, you don't just speak and keep going. You stop, take time to converse a bit; that shows them you are concerned about them, and it makes them feel like they matter. Also, the women are very supportive of one another, especially if you have a child with you or you are elderly. Since we had my grandson with us, we got a lot of attention. The little girls and women would come up to us in the mall and say "Oooo que lindo chico tito." In translation, oh what a nice little guy.

It's almost August now and the three months are coming to an end, so my daughter decided to return to the US and stay at her dad's for a while. I decided to stay on three more months. In order to stay in Peru, you can only do three months at a time and the maximum time is six months unless you have a student or work visa. So she left and I decided to go to Lima and stay for a while. We had flown to Lima and visited Miraflores for a few days after we had been in Peru for about a month as a part of our adventure. It was very beautiful and is right on the coast. That's where most of the tourists go to visit. There is a huge mall that sits right in the side of a mountain. Lima is eight hours from Trujillo, so when we left, we rode a bus and took all of our things. I was sad to see them leave but also excited to see what was coming next, and I was looking forward to some quiet time alone. I made arrangements to stay with a lady named Fany and her family for at least a month, so my daughter and grandson stayed with me overnight, and the next day I took them to the airport to head home. Fany was married and had two teenage boys and a 21-year-old son along with a dog named Surco. This was going to be very different for me, but I had my own bedroom and bathroom all to myself.

After being in Lima for a few days, I had to exit the country as well. I wasn't ready to return to the US just yet so I went to Guayaquil Ecuador for a few days. I really didn't know what to expect, but I was pleasantly surprised. It was a beautiful city and after my flight, my taxi driver took me on a tour of the city and some of the sites. It was very hot there because it is closer to the equator. Had I been thinking, I should have gone to Ecuador from Trujillo instead of Lima because I would have been closer and could have traveled on the bus. I didn't do much on this trip. There was a lady from Maryland that I met while I was there. We shared a couple of meals together and shared stories about our families. I did venture out and check out my surroundings by foot mostly, but I mainly wanted to chill. In order to re-enter Peru I had to have a return flight to the US, and I had until November so I just chose any date, October 26. I flew back into Lima and went through customs and was legal for another three months.

When I returned to Lima, Fany had me going all over the place. I went to birthday parties, baby showers, out to dinner and dancing with friends, you name it, we did it. She has a large family so she included me in everything which really made me feel at home. Their boys could speak and understand English very well and liked watching American TV shows. They loved my pancakes, spaghetti and salmon patties. Some days I would teach her English and other days she would teach me Spanish.

My money was starting to get low so I wanted to find a job, and I started inquiring. I had a lot of skills but the lack of communication was an issue. I worked for a telemarketing company for a couple of days, but that is not for me. Then I applied for an English speaking job and actually got it, but I really didn't like being in Lima, because the weather was terrible. It was at least 10 degrees lower than Trujillo and was rainy and gloomy most of the time. It was very hard to dry your clothes because we hung them up outside. I would walk (for exercise) to the

Wong department store which was over a mile away and the weather made it difficult sometimes. In spite of all the fun things to do, I turned the job down and decided to go back to Trujillo. I made a couple phone calls, said my goodbyes and headed back at the end of August. I took the bus back and literally went from gloom to sunshine. I felt like I was going home again.

I arrived at the bus station that night, Hermes picked me up and Alleen was waiting at home. They wanted me to stay at their house overnight and insisted that I stay in the Peru Mission house which was a large three bedroom apartment that was located near the town center. They let me stay there rent free and wouldn't even let me pay for utilities and said I could stay as long as I like. They didn't know that my money was running low, and I wasn't sure how I was going to make it, but GOD knew and had it all in his hands. I stayed up late, woke up late and some days even took naps. Some of the church family would invite me over for lunch or dinner. I even had a maid once a week. How sweet is that?? My stress level was non existent. I had stopped taking my blood pressure medicine and my blood thinner because I was walking, getting exercise, eating better and getting plenty of rest. During the day I would read my Word and sing praises to almighty GOD for being my protector, my provider and my keeper. I felt fearless and powerful. I had peace, and peace is priceless. I felt loved, accepted and even needed. I was so grateful for this opportunity. It is something that I would have never done on my own, but I was walking in grace, favor, the will of GOD and also obedience to GOD. What a blessing!

About mid- October, I was talking to one of my girl friends on the phone from home, I didn't tell her everything about my concerns. I left out the negative stuff and she stopped me in the middle of our conversation and said, "Why don't you come home?" I went on telling her I was trying to get work and looking forward to making Peru my home. Not telling her that it was hard for me to find a job because of the communication barrier. I remember when I was taking a shower in the first apartment when I first arrived in Peru. I was hearing the word trabajo, which means work. GOD was already letting me know that I wouldn't be working, but he took care of me. She said if you come on back, you can stay with me. I'm never here because I work all the time and my place needs some life in it. I told her that I would think and pray about it and let her know in a couple of days. I called her after a couple of days and had decided that it was time for me to go home. I asked her if she was serious about me staying with her and she said yes, so on October 26th I flew back to the States.

Some of my family and friends didn't understand why I gave up everything to go to a place on my own that I knew nothing about, and on top of that took my daughter and grandson with me. As crazy as I am,

I'm not that crazy. The only reason that I followed through is because GOD heard my cry once again and answered my prayers. That was one of the hardest and best "Trust Me" situations I have ever encountered. I was in complete surrender to HIM. I found out that you don't have to be a millionaire to live like one. He can bless you through people, open doors that you didn't even know existed and make a way out of no way. When I came back to the states, I didn't have much more than what I had in my suitcases, but within 2 months restoration had already begun. You see most of that stuff was just stuff. I realized years ago that as long as GOD gives me strength, if I had it once, I can have it again. Within one year, I had everything that I needed, and some (Proverbs 3: 5-6).

GOOD MORNING SUNSHINE

Good morning Sunshine
what a lovely day
Such a gentle breeze
and the thought of you
Everything's going my way.
Your gentle touch
Your warm embrace
seems to make my heart beat and race.
Soft kisses from your sweet lips
Oooo, I can't resist.
Take care of me Sunshine
Nurture me, protect me, and love me
For if you do this
I'll make sure Spring last forever!

-- Lana Peek

CHAPTER 6

The Boss

Right out of high school, I knew that I wanted to be in fashion, I have always had a love for beautiful clothes. I think I got that from my dad because he was always a spiffy dresser and would coordinate his whole look from head to toe. My dad could only afford to send me to a local community college so I went there for a year and studied Secretarial Science. However, I wasn't the type to sit behind a desk and be confined to one room all day. I felt trapped so I stayed out of school for one year. During that year I worked and saved my money, I applied for a student loan and paid my own way through a business college in Raleigh. I earned an Associate Degree in Fashion Merchandising.

I really wanted to become a Fashion Designer, and I was so good at it during that time. I could look at a garment and know who the designer was. I even took Home Economics in high school and learned how to sew. One of my favorite neighbors who was like a grandmother to me, taught me how to sew, crochet and knit. I even made money making baby blankets, sweaters, etc. Even today, I make scarves for my friends at holiday time. It started out when I was a child; my sister and I had paper dolls and when the tabs would come off of the clothes or the clothes got torn up, we would design our own clothes for the paper dolls. I miss that opportunity because while I was in college, I had a chance to work with some merchandisers out of New York City, but that meant I had to move there. Since I didn't know anyone there and didn't have support from anyone to encourage me to do that, I was afraid to strike out on my own. I ended up in retail management and that lasted for about five years. I started out as an assistant manager and then managed my own store. Sometime later, I realized that I wanted to do hair.

I have been a licensed cosmetologist for more than 30 years. When I finished beauty school I knew I wanted to have my own business. I vowed that my salon would not be like so many others a gossiping, news carrying place. That is a vow that I have kept over the years. Another vow that I made was that I would not be one of those stylists who went from shop to shop and seemed unstable. Well in that case I failed. I worked in a couple of salons in Spring Lake at first to get some experience and learn from some seasoned and master stylists. I went back to my hometown in

1989 because there seemed to be more of a need of a good stylist there. I was forced to open my own salon if I wanted to do business because there were a lot of salons in Moore County, but very few did black hair and those shops were too small, basically a one man shop. The other salon owners would say, "We don't do black hair."

I got tired of hearing that so one day I had to tell one salon owner that I wasn't looking for a salon that did black hair, I just wanted to rent a space from them so that I could do it. I asked my father if he would co-sign a $3,000 loan so I could set up my shop and he did. It was a three year loan and I paid it back in a year and a half. When I first opened, I had clients right away, and that's unheard of. I have been busy ever since. Before I opened I went to a lot of social events and passed out a lot of business cards, introduced myself and got to know a lot of people. There are some clients who have been with me for three generations deep now. Wow! My experience in this business has been up and down. I have had my own salon, and I have worked in other salons and had to move or change locations for various reasons which were sometimes out of my control.

One experience that was so profound to me was in 2009 during the recession. I was working in a salon that I really liked and I loved the people that I was working with, but with businesses closing down, I found myself once again in a situation where I had to move. The salon owner that I was working with felt bad and was concerned that I wouldn't have anywhere to work. I assured her that I would be okay and that I could find somewhere to work, and I went looking for the both of us to have a place together. I found this place; it was beautiful and I wanted it. The building was almost 1400 square feet, it had beautiful hardwood floors, a couple of columns inside and the walls were white and I could paint them any color that I wanted. The building had been newly renovated. I told the owner of the building that I will talk to my partner and if she didn't want it, I would take it and let her know what we decided. I realized what I had just said, but I didn't know how I was going to be able to do that. I was so excited that I went back to my partner and told her about the building but she didn't want to move to Aberdeen.

I was heartbroken and upset. I really wasn't prepared financially at that time and I told God, you know I want it so I need you to make a way. The spirit responded right away and said, "The way has already been made, you walk in it," so things started happening. I was leaving work one day and the Holy Spirit said, "Go and claim the building." I was on my way to do that, but got distracted and was on my way home. I realized it and went back to claim the building and once again, I got side tracked. It took three tries that day. I was almost home when I realized that when I got to the building I didn't claim it, so I turned around and went back. I looked in the alcove and closed my eyes. It was as if I wrapped my arms around the whole building then I claimed it, in the name of Jesus.

Shortly after that, in spite of the fact that there were two other people who were interested in the building, I was able to get it and set it up the way I wanted to. I purchased all the equipment and some furniture from the lady that I had been working with. A friend of mine helped me with some finances. A few family members and a couple of friends helped me set it up. We went in there working 12 hour days for at least three days. It took four days total before I was open for business. We were in a crunch because I wanted it to be ready for Easter and it was.

A few years prior to me acquiring this place, I had already created a name for the salon, picked out pictures according to what I wanted it to look like. I chose paint color samples, the whole nine. Once I got this salon I set it up like I saw it in my imagination. You see I am a firm believer that you have to see something before you see a thing and hold it in your hand. I was there for seven years and had a couple of other people in there working with me until I left to go out of the country. When it was time to go, the same Spirit that told me to claim the building, told me to release it, and I did.

It's so beautiful when God can bless you with something and will use other people to be blessing to you. For a while, I gave clothes away right out of my salon. I just created a corner for it. It had been in my spirit to do it for a while, but I wasn't sure how I would start it. I thought, well, I could easily go through my closet, and I talked to one of the ladies that worked with me and she said she would too. Before we could do that, a friend of mine called me up one day and said, "My lady passed away and I have all these clothes and I don't know what to do with them." I told her to just bring them by. She said it's too many for me to bring, can you come and get them? When I went to pick up the clothes, her living room was filled with them and they filled the inside and the trunk of my mid-size car. I even left some there. I only had two large racks so I had to store some of the clothes in the back until I had room for them, and then of course, I did go through my closet. I knew that it was what GOD intended because he started it. Everytime the racks went low, more people would donate and the racks would fill right back up again. If I needed something for children, I would say, Lord I need some children clothes and they would appear. If I needed some men's clothes, someone would bring them. It was such a blessing to the people. My next step will be to have a building where I will not only give clothes, but also housewares and furniture for people in need. For those like myself who love to change things around a bit, they can bring a table to get a table and that way those who need will still have.

I have always been a giver, and it is always given back to me in so many ways. I have gained things, and I have lost things, and I'm not afraid to take risks. I have found that if it's something you want to do, or if GOD gives you inspiration or ideas, then it has purpose so, don't be afraid. Fear will keep you from doing things, from having things and from being a blessing to other people. I have always been a risk-taker and I have no regrets even in the things that didn't work out because it was a learning experience. I love the freedom that being my own boss has given me. I make my own schedule and I have the freedom to go and do things that I want and need to do. This business has been very rewarding to me and my family, it has allowed us to live a comfortable life. I will never look back on things and say, I should have, would have or could have done anything. Instead I will say, been there, done that, even wrote a book about it!

You Gotta Have Faith

Faith is the substance of things hoped for
and the evidence of things not seen
You gotta have faith

When you're going through something
and you don't know what to do
Just give it to Jesus and he will see you through
You gotta have faith

I know it's hard to trust
when you just don't understand
You must realize, God has his own plan
You gotta have faith

When there's no food on the table
When your friends walk away
When there's no work insite
Throw your hands up and say
Lord I trust you, please make a way!
You gotta have faith

They say weeping may endure for a night
Just get a good grip and hold on tight
Joy will come in the morning light
Just keep the faith!!

--Lana Peek

Life's Journey

Through my life's journey, I have learned so many things about myself, other people and my relationship with GOD. I've learned that truly some people are in our lives for a reason, a season or a lifetime. Relationships come and go and the negative ones we have to let go. Sometimes we get involved with other peoples' problems that don't even belong to us that may cause us to suffer and that battle is not even ours. I've learned that GOD truly does love us and HE will bless us even in the midst of our sin. HE will fight for us as long as we are in the right; obedience is better than sacrifice. HE is all that I need. HE is my friend, my keeper, my provider, my everything. HE made me in HIS own image, and HE gives me HIS power through the Holy Spirit. I've learned to forgive and forget things so they won't hold me back. I'm moving forward, "keep it moving," I always say. The things that I have been through and experienced, the good and the bad, have made me who I am, and for that I am very grateful. I'm trying to live my life here on earth so that I will have my eternal reward in heaven. I have decided that I won't settle for less, and the ideas and thoughts that GOD gives me are for a reason. I have to do all that I can and HE will bless as I go and do. HE will put HIS super on my natural and make anything possible. If I can imagine or see it in the Spirit, then I can hold it in my hand. It is so!!

About the Author

Lana Peek has always been a visionary and a dreamer, that is what has kept her motivated and encouraged over the years. She has always had a love for people and life in general with the hope of making a difference in this world. She is very involved in community service. She has an Associates Degree in Fashion Merchandising with retail management experience. She has been a licensed Cosmetologist for more than 30 years. She is a certified Life Coach and is also in ministry. She is an entrepreneur and a successful business woman. Every job or career has always been focused on others by giving the best customer service and care with the spirit of excellence. God has blessed her with many gifts and talents which include; writing, painting, drawing, singing, sewing, crocheting, knitting, Interior design, floral arrangements and anything else creative. She has one beautiful daughter, a three- year- old grandson and a two- year- old granddaughter with special needs.

If you find yourself in need of help with some of the issues in your own life or need some direction, as a certified life coach she can help you navigate through them. You can reach out to her through her Facebook page or email; lana.peek@yahoo.com

Made in the USA
Middletown, DE
18 March 2022

62732052R00056